GROW DEEP

NOT JUST TALL

by Karen Kaiser Clark

Illustrations by Larry W. Anderson

Published in the United States of America by
The Center for Executive Planning, Inc.

First Printing: March 1984
Second Printing: March 1985
Third Printing: March 1986
Fourth Printing: March 1987
Fifth Printing: October 1987

Library of Congress Catalog Card Number: 84-070372

Inquiries and orders should be addressed to:
The Center for Executive Planning, Inc.
13119 Heritage Way
Suite 1200
St. Paul, Minnesota 55124
612/454-1163

CONTENTS

Dedicated to my husband
and best friend, Lou, and
our children, Kelli and Kevin

Preface

Humans have always searched for an oracle, a source of wise counsel and prophetic vision. Oracles can take any form. In this book it is an old, gnarled, oak tree that speaks to us. This wise and weathered spirit has lived through many seasons. He continues to GROW DEEP NOT JUST TALL. Openly he shares the gift of who he is with those who choose to listen.

Our culture teaches us to be logical and sequential in our thinking. Growth is often perceived as a progression from infancy, childhood, adolescence and finally into adulthood. We are encouraged to look outside ourselves to find truth and strength. We engage in competitive comparisons to define our levels of success and value. The Tree offers a different and balancing perception.

Growing deep, like wisdom, extends beyond objective, critical forms of thinking. Inches, seasons, even years address only the externals of real growth. As The Tree cautions, "Look beyond the surface of first impressions." The seasons in this book do not necessarily parallel the stages of human growth. Reach deep within your core for light and warmth. The Tree affirms, "We are each so much more than what some reduce to measuring."

This little book is filled with life and hope. It does not give answers. Rather, it offers invitations to you, My Friend, to journey with The Tree and to grow through each season in your own way. Search with your heart for what is real in each page. The seeds of new beginnings are hidden everywhere; in the words, in the drawings and in you. Growth takes time and patience to nurture into fullness. Risk letting go and rediscover your own magic. The gift of choice is yours. Will you choose to live fully and to GROW DEEP NOT JUST TALL? The Tree patiently awaits your decision.

THE SEASONS OF LIFE
WEAVE A PATTERN

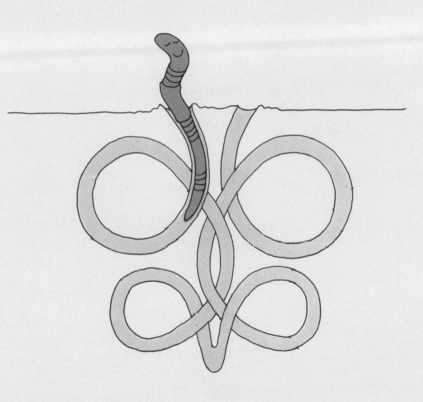

Oh, my friend, I am so glad you have come again. I have missed you in the seasons that have separated us. Even trees get lonely and long to be remembered. We share so much in common, you and I.

Come close now. Let me feel the softness of your cheek against my trunk. Trace your sensitive fingers in the grooves of my bark. Let us always touch one another in gentle ways and nourish each other's growth.

So many others passed me by as the seasons slipped into one another. I waited patiently for someone to discover me. Last spring you paused and noticed me. You saw something special that all the others missed.

We laughed and cried and found joy and shelter in one another. I discovered a specialness in you. It is the child in you, my friend, that so delights me. Hold fast to that magic center of who you are.

Hush now and rest on me. It is good to have you close and sometimes . . . quiet. We all need to be heard and I have treasured gifts to share with you. Listen with your heart, my friend, and I will speak to you with who I am.

I have lived through many seasons. One blended into the other like the strands of your braids. It is not possible to separate them without spoiling how beautifully they flow together.

We too are a blend of so many pieces. Some of our needs are out of season. Some of our wounds still ache to be healed. So many buds await to be blossomed.

We move through the seasons together. Each cycles at their own pace. Each is a part of the other. In time a pattern appears, woven by the choices we have made.

Like wind rustling my leaves and bending my boughs, life flows from season to season. Even in the darkness it moves on, straining for the light. Unfailingly, the night gives in to dawn.

Life is ever changing, always new. Many yesterdays slip into today. Yet, each sunrise offers a fresh new day. Tomorrow can never be now and for one of us . . . may never be known.

Make the most of your moments and remember,
   Change is not merely necessary for life,
      Life is change . . .
         Growth is optional . . .
         Choose wisely . . .

Growing up just happens. Growing deep we must choose. It requires us to vulnerably open ourselves to the possibilities for growth. It calls us to extend our roots and to reach out our branches. It leads us to touch and to be touched by the whole of life. It dares us to embrace every moment and live it fully.

If we choose to grow deep, we must live through the cold winter as well as the warm spring. We must learn to celebrate the letting go of autumn as well as the fullness of summer.

It is not easy to grow in this way. Be assured, my friend, it is all right to be frightened. It takes courage to live fully. Everyone is afraid at times.

Few seek the depths of their potential. Most are too cautious to risk growing deep. They will not accept the growing pains and the uncertainty of change. They run from opportunities. They pretend they have no options. They choose to stay in their same old ruts. They may be miserable but at least their patterns are predictable. Oh what a price they choose to pay for supposed security.

There are no goblins in the forest, my friend. But there are real ghosts that haunt our growing deep. They howl spooky thoughts and even frighten some to death.

Their names are, Old Excuses, Rigid Routine, and Narrow Vision. They are the ghosts of fear. You must face them one by one. If you don't, the ruts you walk in will deepen daily. Remember . . . the only difference between a rut and a grave is the depth of the hole. Step aware-fully.

In our seasons of separation, I have grown. The fullness of last summer drew my branches higher and wider. In autumn my roots let loose of sandy soil and now reach farther than ever. Over the long winter my patience grew as I watched and waited hopefully for your return. Oh, it is so good to have you close again.

You too have grown. Your arms reach farther around me. I feel the tickle of your hair a bit higher on my trunk. You, my friend, are growing up.

The child in you, that magic center, is also growing deep. How wonderful! It sparkles with curiosity. I see it in your eyes. I hear it in your laughter. I taste it in your tears. You are wonder-full!!!

There is no other in the world quite like you, my dear friend. You are unequaled, precious ... and still prized by your own self. Hold fast to these perceptions. They are magic in a world of constant, outward competition.

We are each so much more than what some reduce to measuring. So little of me is perceived in the calculated distance to my highest branch. The rings within my core and the things to which I am rooted, reveal so much more of who I am. Those who live their lives only growing ... up ... do not grasp these deeper perceptions.

Existing and living are not the same. To live fully is to grow deep, not just tall. These are the seeds of wisdom I long to nurture with you, my friend, as we grow through the seasons together.

IT IS SPRING

THE SEASON OF NEW BEGINNINGS AND OF GROWTH

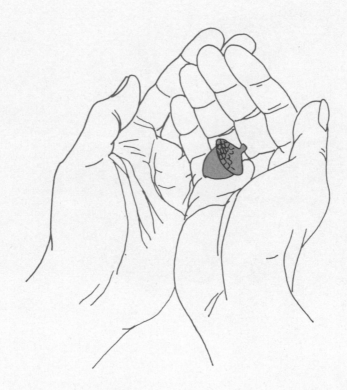

The chilly days are warmer and the stream is free of ice. Polliwogs are sprouting legs. Eggs are cracking. Birds are coming home to budding trees. The brown of winter is greening.

A seed bursts and the ground is split. A single blade of grass begins the meadow. New life comes from shedding old skins and pressing through the darkness toward the light. Spring is the season of new beginnings and of growth. It is a time for recalling our first rooting and choosing how we will grow.

One spring long ago, I began as a tiny acorn, no bigger than the one nestled in your palm. As a tiny seedling I eased my slender roots into the soil and was nourished. Now feel how rooted I am with our earth. Feel how cradled you are in the slope of my trunk. From the moment of our birth we are interdependent . . . even long before that moment.

Everywhere there are tiny seeds; in the air, in the soil, in each of us, my friend. Life is playing hide-and-seek everywhere we turn. Let's discover it, nourish it and grow.

In our early beginnings we must not be too quickly or too often uprooted. New life is a delicate gift. It thrives in the presence of warm sun and soft rain. It blossoms in the caress of tender breezes. It delights in the humor of winking stars.

But the pattern for few is so smooth. Life can be cold and unfair. In search of nourishment, many have had to struggle through crevices that were cruel and hard. They were offered so little and sometimes . . . no support. Edging their way, so often alone, somehow they barely survive.

Their fragile roots yanked and torn so many times, it is a wonder they ever endured. It is also of little wonder . . . some are now . . . so afraid . . . to trust life.

Others grow beyond hard beginnings. The biting cold nips most of their blossoms. The bitter wind snaps many of their boughs. Yet, incredibly they hold fast. Tenaciously they anchor. They grow deep in the midst of confusion. Like all, they were hurt and at times . . . even crushed. Yet somehow they do more than survive.

They choose to grow through adversity and to risk reinvesting in life. They know life is unfair yet continue to believe that love is far stronger than hate. In the midst of their crises, these creative survivors, find a strength that is powerfully gentle. It flows from their center with life-giving warmth, like sap pouring all through my core. They respond to its presence and hold on with hope.

My friend, what is real cannot always be seen with our eyes, touched with our hands, or enframed in the things we call words. Our hearts can know truths our heads can never hold. Troubled times can strengthen us and be our greatest gifts. Learn from these sensitive survivors.They grow deep, not just tall. They are believers in life.

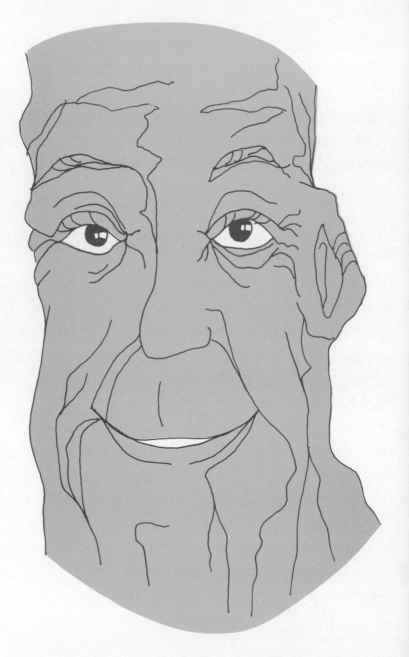

Believers in life are creative. They look for lessons to be learned in all that happens. They pull life from every day of every season. They freely offer who they are and what they have. They sink their roots deep in soil that nurtures life and are not afraid to risk asking for help.

Believers in life choose not to be bitter. Nor do they abandon life or run away. They listen for laughter, for music, and the source of light and life. They cherish what is real and find no shame in imperfection. And oh, how they strive to forgive . . . those who hurt them . . . themselves . . . and life itself. Yet they do not forget painful memories. They know that to forget would invite repeating the painful past.

They weather the windstorms and still can smile. They watch for the sunrise and search for the stars. Their faithful, quiet courage invite us to hold on and to hope. Their active presence speaks eloquently of an unconquerable spirit that chooses life . . . again . . . and . . . again.

If April showers bring May flowers, they also bring the worms. Those wiggling, slithering creatures are the tillers of the soil. Perhaps to us not pretty . . . but their mothers claim they are. It is true that we find what we look for . . . even in worms, my friend.

Remember the chill that raced up your spine, when you stepped on a worm bare-footed? Remember the thrill of then feeling one crawl, when the fear eased away as you held one?

Not all that we face can be changed or accepted. But few fears are released . . . until we face them.

Lightening can be frightening. It shatters the quiet of a calm spring evening. It rips jagged gashes in the night. It can be terrifying, especially when we are alone. We freeze motionless, stiffened with anxiety and the anticipation of the thunder sure to follow. We feel isolated, anxious and afraid.

Lightening can be brightening. Sometimes the light it brings, helps us to see things more clearly. Its flash fills the darkness with enlightening insights. It confirms the presence of those close beside us. They may be even nearer than we imagined before the storm. The air clears. The breeze cools. We feel refreshed, comforted and renewed.

Spring storms bring mixed blessings. The lightening can be frightening . . . or . . . brightening. Remember, my friend, whenever we lose we gain. Whenever we gain we lose. Discover the gifts of the lightening.

Nests are sheltering places. My feathered friend built one in the support of my branches. Last spring she placed her tiny eggs there. She trusted me to hold them safe. In their time they hatched and now all have gone. Nests have no locks or latches.

Her nest is still here and I will hold it for her faithfully. Others have found it a warm resting place in her absence. She wouldn't mind. I hope she will return, to nest and sing and fly free again.

Weave your nests in safe places, my friend. Entrust them to those who will not drop you. Rebuild your nests with new grasses and mend the brokenness. Return to those who help you bring life to new beginnings.

IT IS SUMMER

THE SEASON OF
FULLNESS
AND OF GROWTH

Life surges in the core of my trunk and in the tiniest veins in my leaves. Securely rooted and bursting with life, we strive to give our world who we are. At peak moments when all is going our way, we may even foolishly believe . . . we are full grown.

Summer is a joyful time. It is warm and rich, bright and green. Most see only this side of summer. You must see more if you choose to grow deep. For in this season of fullness and of growth, there is always the balance . . . incompleteness. Few accept both halves of the whole.

Growth never completes itself. Nor does love. Nor do we. In our reaching toward completeness we affirm our imperfection. Time pushes us to grow beyond momentary arrivals. Life presses toward greater meanings.

The sun may shine longer in the summer but the moon still touches every day.

When my leaves thirst for water, they wrinkle. The clouds do not always answer with rain. Sometimes they cannot. Sometimes they will not. When my thirst continues, I call to the stream or to the morning dew. No one cloud holds all that can quench me.

My friend, it is unfair to expect others to guess when you are thirsty. Make your needs known. Accept that others will not always answer your requests. Sometimes they cannot. Sometimes they will not. No one holds all that can quench you. Nor is it anyone's task to complete your happiness or to fill your emptiness.

Acknowledging needs can be frightening, for the voices of the ghosts of fear are very seldom quiet. When rejection rubs raw our vulnerablility, they howl gleefully,

> "See, we told you, fool! Don't
> trust! Don't need! Others
> seek only to betray you!"

Face the sources of those scary voices. They lead to loneliness, isolation and a hollow sense of self. Grow deep and far beyond them, my friend. Other voices with different faces call to you.

Gradually reveal your needs to those who truly care. If you will not, your needs may go unnoticed by those near you. Then silent needs turn into anger. Anger becomes depression. Who then is the cause of the sadness?

Listen and respond selectively to the voices that call to you. Look carefully for thirst so well hidden. We need balance . . . not perfection . . . to live life in abundance. To give and to receive lead to fullness.

The sun shines long and hot in summer. Tuck every ray of every day safe inside your memory. No season lasts forever. Wise are those who savour what is treasureable.

Lean back with me and look up. See the splendid parade of fluffy, fat clouds slipping in and out of fantastic creations. Nurture the gift of imagination's magic wand. Relish the greatness of simple pleasures.

Watch a spider spin a web.
Count freckles on a frog.
Find a world inside an anthill.
Taste a raindrop. Hug a dog.

Whistle with a blade of grass.
See fireflies at night.
Watch a butterfly emerge.
Smell a flower. Fly a kite.

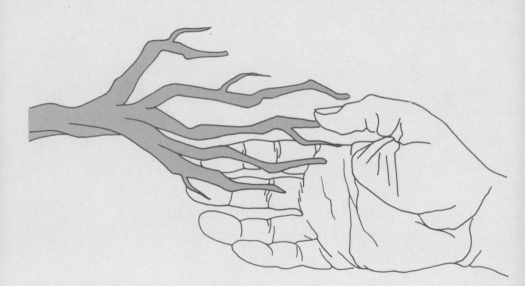

What a joy it is to share some of our roots in common. It enlivens our sense of connectedness. It affirms our being important, special parts of one another.

Let us be sure though, my friend, that our roots do not become entangled. Life-giving relationships are free of binding manipulations, resentments and pressing expectations. Spontaneity is refreshing and essential.

There must be no measuring in our giving and receiving with one another. Those who give genuinely never make us feel the weight of the hand they reach out to us. Those who receive graciously acknowledge being deeply touched, not overwhelmed.

Openly sharing blossoms, when we are solidly rooted. Love flourishes, when we reach out . . . and let go.

It is good to be together. This warm summer day is all the more lovely when we are sharing it. Let us be sure though, my friend, not to be exclusive. We must carefully uproot any hint of possessiveness. Left untended those weeds will choke life from our friendship.

Our roots must be channeled to reach beyond just you and me. We own no one. Each of us is on loan and for such a little time. Our strength and support must be grounded in others as well. We must never suppose that either is the completion of the other. My friend, the day may come when we will not see the sun rise, standing side-by-side.

There are special moments to be known in our times apart from one another. Do not fear them. Grow through them. They will make our coming home to one another all the richer. Go now to the stream. She has nourished me faithfully season after season. I would like the two of you to know one another. You are each so precious to me.

The stream speaks powerfully in moving, symbolic ways. Listen attentively and look beyond the surface of first impressions. Like all we meet, the stream has lessons to teach . . . if we are open.

See how she eases her way at night and day. She gains control by trying not to control and flows with the strength of the current. Even boulders that fall in her path do not stop her. She finds courses around them and sometimes . . . straight through them.

Those same boulders that once threatened to drain her strength and divert her direction, have led to the beauty of her contours.

The stream is like a sculptor who chisels away all that is unreal and unleashes the beauty tucked inside.

See how she receives what is given, even ugliness, and how she restores and renews? Rolled over and over, broken branches become graceful driftwood. Sharp bits of glass are tumbled until they wash a-shore like harmless dots of rainbows in the sand. Over many seasons, rough rocks are smoothed into thin, flat pebbles that make champion wave-skippers. Even her water that runs cold is turned into musical rhythms to warm the hearts of those who listen.

Like the stream, we too must learn to reshape and to recreate. We must chip away and release what conceals our real selves.

Jump out to that old rock in the stream. If you miss . . . you'll get wet . . . but you'll dry. If the breeze chills you, press yourself against the rock. Feel the warmth he shares with you, from having stood all day in the hot sun. Do you understand? Even rocks have gifts to offer.

Toss a line in the stream. Hear the "plunk" of your bait as it dives into the water. Watch the ripples circle wider and wider. Little things can have rippling effects. Do not underestimate the power of a brief encounter, my friend.

Let loose any concern for a trophy catch. Enjoy, but do be attentive should you get a nibble. Some only hint of their presence but long to be caught and reeled in.

To know summer is to live the season fully. In our eagerness for wholeness we must embrace our brokenness. Everyone hurts, my friend. Be gentle.

You see so easily my lush branches, my sturdy bark and my shiny leaves. You listen for the meanings in my words. I feel admiration in your eyes. Come closer now and know me. Touch the gnarls on my limbs. See the hole in my trunk. Your big strong friend is also . . . broken.

Some turned away when they saw my woundedness. Others pretended not to see. The squirrels accepted these parts of me. They scampered lightly along my twisted limbs. They never teased or shamed me. When I invited them, they carefully crawled within my hollowed trunk. They made in it . . . a home.

My friend, perhaps our greatest fear is of being fully known . . . or is it of being . . . never known? I know our deepest longing is for home.

Home is not a place. It is something that happens to us. We know we are home when we cease hiding our twisted limbs, our hollowed trunks, and our dreams and hopes and fears. We come home when we are openly received and accepted. At home we are no longer frightened of who we are and some of our loneliness is settled.

The greatest of all gifts to offer . . . is home. The greatest of all gifts to receive . . . is home. It is seeing and accepting one's fullness and incompleteness. It is inviting and empowering one another to grow. Real intimacy is a home-coming celebration. It is a time of fullness and of growth. It draws us closer toward risking . . . letting go.

IT IS AUTUMN

THE SEASON OF
LETTING GO
AND OF GROWTH

The shadows fall longer and come earlier in the day. Birds glide in patterns like the point of an arrow, leaving their nests far behind. Chestnut-brown cattails sway in the breeze, waving farewell to the summer. Acorns are dropping and a gold harvest moon whispers, "Autumn."

This season is as unpredictable as is life. One day it is hot. The next day pelting rain chills us to our roots. Autumn is the season of letting go and of growth. It is a time for redefining who we are. It reminds us we hold nothing forever . . . even what we believe . . . we cannot live without.

The seed that burst in spring grew to fullness in the summer. Now the brilliant autumn colors hint of brown. Like falling leaves mirrored by the stream, we see our real selves by letting go.

On hot autumn days we slip back into summer. It is hard to accept the sun is fading. Now is the time for one last dip in the stream. Her chilly water will remind you . . . today's heat is temporary.

Kneel down if you dare. You might tremble with the shivers and your teeth may even chatter. In time your chickenflesh and goosebumps disappear. Might it have been easier, just to jump in all at once?

Loosen your braid and let it dangle in the stream. It takes time to unwrinkle the kinks in your hair. The longer in the healing stream . . . the easier it will smooth.

It takes time to smooth the snarls in our lives. That first step towards unknotting feels like plunging into ice. We clench our fists in anger. We stiffen furrowed brows. Then one finger at a time, one tangle . . . then another . . . . we unravel wrinkled pieces one by one.

The stream is speckled with yellow and red. A spunky, spotted sandpiper runs along her banks. It stops abruptly, tilts its head and seems to listen. Then its neck snaps upright and the spindly, little legs dash again.

Listen! The stream is beckoning waving branches overhead. She sings reassurance to the leaves that still fear falling:

"I will not take your colors from you. I seek only to reflect your loveliness. The closer you approach me, the more vividly you will see yourselves. I will openly receive you. Then gracefully we will flow downstream together."

It is frightening to let go, a little less so when we are faithfully reassured. It is hard to believe, that another seeks only to reflect our splendidness. It is harder still, to accept a mirrored-image of ourselves as truly lovely. Yet, what is loving, if not the willingness to commit one's self to another's discovering their beauty?

We do not lose ourselves in loving. We affirm and cherish uniqueness. The stream is still the stream. The leaf is still the leaf. They gracefully flow downstream one with one.

My family of squirrels are busy but they always have time to play. They remind me, "Life is more than intensity. Loosen up. Come play and have fun."

They chase each other round my trunk and leap to branches that barely hold them. They chatter, laugh and tickle me. They are such a joy! Today one flicked a smile and quipped, "Those who laugh . . . last!"

Hundreds of acorns now apron my trunk and the squirrels sense this signal of autumn. Between games of tag they hide them, according to some mystical plan. How can they remember where each one is buried? They only smiled when I asked them. Some secrets aren't for sharing.

I wonder if the squirrels know the secret of my beginning. Was I one who was hidden and perhaps forgotten? How true it is . . . if brought to life, tiny seeds can become even greater seed-bearers.

The moon edges earlier into evening and lingers on longer into morning. The bright sun of weeks ago is now illusive. It feels farther away and cooler. The air is crisp. The scent of autumn is unmistakable. Nothing seems the same. Everywhere life is changing.

The forest is being transformed. Trees are losing their green surfaces. Leaf by leaf, real colors are bleeding through. The colors were always there, only hidden.

Oaks and maples, aspens, elms. Listen to some of them argue! Our differences have become obvious as green masks are peeled away. Some will not accept the realness. The source of their anger is the ghost of Narrow Vision saying,
     "Why can't you do . . . and be . . . like me!"
They do not choose to hear the Source of Life saying,
     "Dare to be different . . . become you.
          The glory of this season is
          a harmony of contrast."

Autumn brings a multitude of changes. At times they are too quickly, even shockingly imposed. The drop of just one single degree, and the fragilness of life is snapped in two. The newness all around us can be nearly overwhelming. Yet the changes deep within, can be the hardest to accept . . . especially those over which we sense such little control.

We oaks are perceived as sturdy and resourceful. We are strong. My friend, don't be fooled. Change is hard for us too. Just look at my limbs filled with leaves I barely recognize. Their green is all gone. These new rusty, copper colors are such a contrast. All too soon they will reach their peak and I have to begin to let them go.

It is one challenge to acquaint myself with these changing, withered pieces of who I am. It is quite another task to let them go. Most years I have held them long into winter. Perhaps now that you are with me, I will let them go a little sooner.

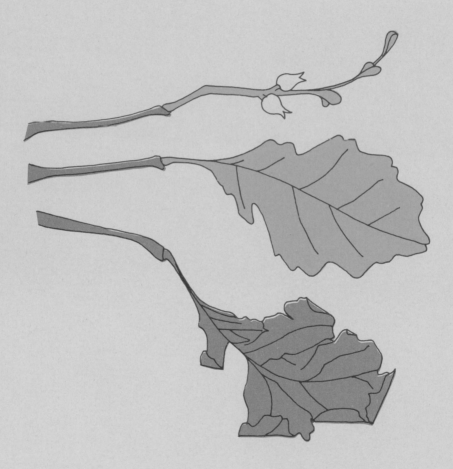

Multicolored leaves weave a quilted, patchwork covering on the ground. They are fun for you to gather and to jump in playfully. How I love to hear your laughter and watch you toss them in the air. Some brush your cheek in falling and hint of greater meanings. Continue searching with your heart to discover what is real. My leaves are more than leaves, my friend.

In spring you saw my leaves as tiny buds. Did your heart see them as my hopes and dreams of fresh, new life unfolding? In summer you saw them waving in the breeze. Did you see them as fingers inviting you nearer? Could you hear them whispering my needs? Now my leaves are brittle and you see their real colors. They are my tears overflowing with many meanings.

As unmatched as the leaves from different trees, our tears are very personal expressions. If you choose to grow deep, learn the language of tears. Everyone speaks them, but with different accents and meanings, according to how we have been taught . . . or allowed . . . to expose ourselves.

Leaves fall at different times. So do tears. Some allow them only in certain seasons. Others try forever to withhold them, perhaps fearful of exposing barren branches. Others drop them constantly and clutter those around them with self pity.

The slightest breeze can twist a narrow stem and a single trembling leaf trickles free. So too, a thought, a scene or a melody can loose a single tear. As unknown as the source of the breeze, the reasons for our tears can be as unexplainable. Tears confirm our rootedness in life beyond ourselves. They express our capacities to care . . . to care enough about something . . . or for someone . . . to cry.

The tears of those who grow deep are shed at different times but always in moments filled with meanings. They surface on occasions of great joy and heated anger, of rejection and of coming home, in times of loss and of reconciliation. Whenever we are deeply touched, filled with love . . . or emptiness . . . our tears can shower down like leaves whirled in a windstorm.

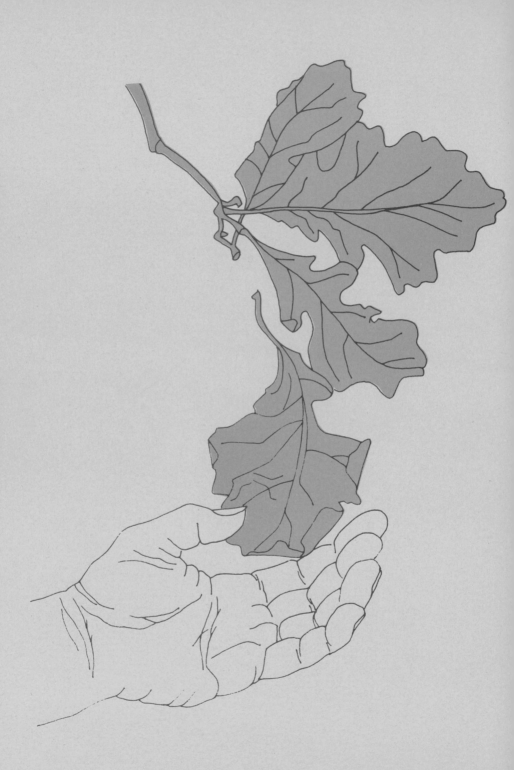

The stongest, tallest trees may have the most leaves and tears to shed. Standing alone, under the cover of darkness, some fall silently in bunches. Perhaps the loneliest of all are those who have no one in whose presence they feel free to weep.

Those who grow deep, no longer hide from tears. Having felt them streaming down their reddened cheeks and knowing intimately the salty taste of loss, they rediscover something of themselves in those who can stand alone. No longer do they back away when another's eyes start blinking. Quietly and openly they offer a priceless gift . . . the gift of simple presence of one who truly cares. There may be no words, not even a touch . . . only tears. Releasing them can bring healing, cleansing . . . even joy.

Tears wash away our illusions of magnified isolation. What is most personal is also universal. We all have tears tucked deep inside. Oh, my friend, it is not our place to take each other's tears away. Yet, venturing to share them can be a bonding expression of trust. If I let loose my tears with you . . . remember . . . I am entrusting you with real pieces of who I am. Do be care - full.

There is a scurry of activity throughout the forest. Tiny insects are burrowing deep into the cooling soil, hoping to escape the killing frost. Waves of birds are drifting farther south, responding to the voice that maps the way. Even at night preparations are being made. Tireless raccoons stuff themselves, storing fat for their long winter sleep.

Change is everywhere. Just look at my branches! Suddenly they are ablaze, filled with swarms of vibrant, monarch butterflies. The caterpillars that ate the leaves of summer have become life transformed. With just the right breeze, they arise in a fluttering, orange cloud and head for warmer places, thousands of miles away. At winter's end, they will return to pollinate the flowers of those same plants and scurry of new beginnings will fill the forest.

Life cycles through each season, weaving patterns, blending change. We too must prepare for colder days ahead. No longer can we depend on the sun alone to warm us. My friend, it is not only wise . . . it is essential . . . to prepare, for what in time, will surely come.

Feel how sharp the wind has become. It orchestrates the trees in scratchy tones as the leaves scrape one another. Few remain compared to just a few short weeks ago. Most lay heaped on the ground . . . wrinkled, brittle bits of summer past. Cold autumn rains settle the thick, airy layers into a soggy, brown blanket of molding leaves. Yielding themselves to the moisture, they become nourishment for seasons yet to come. Life is never lost, only changed. Each season nourishes the next.

The heavy scent of dampness weights the air. Only an occasional drizzle breaks the monotony of dull gray clouds and the murky silence of hazy, birdless skies. This is a dreary time.

There is a sense of gloom and depression on days like these. Moments feel lifeless. Now is the time to recall those warm, sunny days we tucked safe inside our memories. No day lasts forever . . . even this one. We must await another season, discover a new dimension of growing deep. Be patient, my friend, winter is coming.

IT IS WINTER

THE SEASON OF
PATIENCE
AND OF GROWTH

Wrapped in frozen stillness, the forest is quiet and cold. These early morning hours are very long. It seems the sun has overslept and that the night will never end. Waiting is a lesson each must learn. It is not easy to be patient in the dark.

A glimmer of light peeks above the faint horizon. Ever so slowly the sun ascends. Gradually a new day is unveiled. Dawn always comes . . . but in this season, it is delayed.

Growth may even go unnoticed as it slowly, oh so slowly, yields life. Growth takes time to nurture and to realize, my friend. Do not force . . . or it may die before its time.

Winter is the season of patience and of growth. It is the time to learn that life will not be hurried. We cannot spin the dials of cycled seasons. Live fully in this moment, for it will not ever come to you again. Patience is not passive. It is the rawest kind of courage. It opens us to living every moment. Grow deep these wintry days and look within for light and warmth.

Gracefully falling snowflakes dance with winter's winds. Delicately they cloak me. Even my tiniest twigs are gloved in white. A thick blanket of snow is tucked around the base of my trunk. Snuggled safe beneath winter's wardrobe, sleep the seeds of new beginnings. This is a time to pause, to rest and to be quiet. This season brings forth life in different forms.

The stream is laced with fringes of ice crystals. In the weeks to come her banks will reach for one another. Her ripples will flatten stiff, into solid sheets of ice. Then the land and stream will join . . . one with one.

Squirrels will scamper safely on her surface. They will find new ways to play in winter's cold. A sense of humor is essential in every season. We may have days of mere survival but there is no real living without laughter.

Accumulated snowfalls can be unbearable. The weight of winter presses hard upon me. Some collapse beneath the heavy load. I know, in time I too will reckon with that moment. Now I strain and long for patience to endure. If I were not deeply rooted, perhaps I'd run away. I fear I cannot hold up for much longer.

Biting, bitter, brutal winds lash and whistle through me. It is too cold for tears to even surface. My bark is frozen stiff and winter feels . . . forever. Outside me life is harsh and sometimes even . . . cruel.

In these lonely, painful moments I question . . . why . . . and wonder. I hear the ghosts of fear begin to howl. At times I doubt the wisdom of choosing to endure. There seems to be no reason to hold on. What value is a skeleton . . . that reflection of me shadowed in the moonlight?

My friend, the memory of you comforts me . . . but now I must confront my own aloneness. I must journey deep within and rediscover . . . life . . . I once knew flowing through my center. Its warmth and light will comfort, though may be hard to feel or see. Patience takes more courage than I imagined in the summer.

Hidden memories sometimes surface if we venture toward our center. Some constantly keep running to avoid those confrontations. It takes courage to stand still in winter's quiet.

The indelible marks of memories are like the furrows in my bark. Some deeply grooved images leave rough impressions of life and love. I know . . . for long ago I remember shivering alone. I heard voices coming near me. I willingly reached out, hoping to share and to care. They were unkind. They splintered my branches and snapped them from my trunk. Confused, I questioned . . . what I did . . . to elicit such unkindness.

Many seasons passed before I shared my guarded secret. Only then did I discover, I owned no cause for shame. I was innocently wounded. Those who tore and used my wood, built a fire to warm themselves. They showed no interest or compassion for the hurt that they imposed. Perhaps some even reasoned that a tree would have no feelings.

We all have broken pieces in our past, my trusted friend. Each has known the pierce of innocence betrayed. Perceive such times as unfair prunings . . . that still . . . can bring forth life. Hold on to roots that nourish and continue on to heal.

Colors seldom go unnoticed in this season. Blue skies contrast clearly, the typical wintry grays. Bright red cardinals stand out strikingly when perched in snowy trees. Against the white backdrop of winter even tiny bits of color catch our eye.

Sounds are heard more sharply in the cold. They ring crisp with crystal clearness and call for our attention. Spiraling icicles tinkle like winter windchimes. Every season has its theme song, but if there are too many noises, the music can't be heard.

The bleakness of this season exposes much we take for granted and even miss. The neglected signs of life become apparent from a distance. Winter heightens our awareness of the little things that give life greater meaning.

I hear the crunch of snow off in the distance. Slowly guarded steps come closer to me. A flash of panic overwhelms me. I remember those who hurt me in the past. Now more cautiously I question who is coming.

A deer timidly approaches. It seems more frightened and more lonely than I have ever been. It is good to have its company and not be alone. I want the deer to stay, perhaps even to come closer. Standing still I hold back . . . and wait.

The hardest part of patience is actively restraining, when every fiber in us aches to say or do. If we are unwilling to wait, we miss those who wish to share but who cannot give themselves all at once. If we impose with our impatience, we rob others of the time they need to grow. We may even frighten some away with best intentions.

Patience is a law of life and a measure of real love. It is a test of true devotion and of faithfulness. Waiting can be the hardest, yet the wisest thing to do. Few things of great value happen suddenly. Life and love can begin in a moment but deepen and mature through many seasons.

The brightness of the sun reflects most brilliantly at noon on snowy days. Despite the blinding glare the cold still threatens to demand my full attention. I choose instead to focus on the sun.

She still stands at a distance, yet her rays reach out for me. We both ignore the wind and cold that nudge to be acknowledged. We yearn for one another and joyfully embrace. A filigree of frost sparkles like icy diamonds along my barren branches. Her touch begins to thaw my frozen limbs. Like a breath breathed into a dwindling fire, her rays stir life within me. In this one single moment, I feel chilled and warmed, nakedness and dazzling ecstacy.

Moments are filled with a mixture of contrasting realities. My friend, we have no power to control when the sun will shine or how the wind will blow in any season. We do have . . . great power . . . to choose or to let go of our perceptions of them both.

Those who grow deep cease pretending they have no options. They embrace sometimes painfully . . . often courageously . . . what brings light and love alive.

Icicles drip. The stream trickles free. There is a sooth-
ing rhythm in the melting of the cold. The white of the
snow slowly disappears. The frozen ground is soften-
ing and the tillers of the soil begin to stretch. Beneath
the layers of my fallen leaves, sprout the roots of a
wild rose. There is no winter harsh enough to withhold the promise of spring.

Oh, how I miss you, my friend. Another season is
nearing and I long to celebrate its new beginnings
with you. I recall the softness of your cheek against
my trunk and the tenderness of your fingers tracing
the grooves in my bark. I feel the laughter and the
wonder we unleashed in one another. I hear the
music of the seasons that we shared. We have
touched one another in gentle ways and have
nourished each other's growth. Now I watch and wait
patiently for your return. Yet . . .

You are here . . . as I am with you . . . and forever we
will be. There is no distance or measure of time that
can separate the freeing bond of love. Rich with
memories to warm us and with hope to brighten the
darkest night, let us continue to live fully and to risk
growing deep not just tall.

Listen with your heart, my friend. There is magic in
this moment . . . and in you.

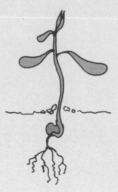

IT IS NOW
THE SEASON
FOR GROWTH

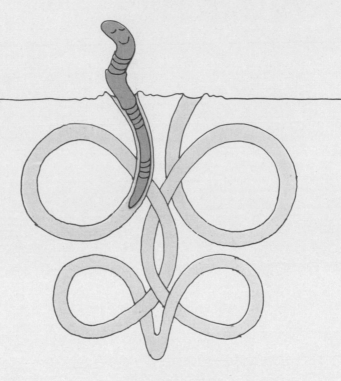

WILL YOU,
MY FRIEND?

AUTHOR

Karen Kaiser Clark is as warm and approachable as she appears. A former teacher, Karen now lectures and conducts seminars internationally for business and industry, hospitals and private organizations, schools and universities. A popular keynote speaker addressing the broad area of human relations, Karen has earned her reputation as a real professional who  shares who she is as well as what she has learned. She graduated with honors from Western Michigan University and went on to do graduate work in psychology at the Universities of Michigan and Minnesota. She served many years as a consultant for the Minnesota Department of Education and has conducted workshops for school administrators in as far away places as The Philippine Islands and Okinawa. As President of The Center for Executive Planning, Karen recently published her second book, Grow Deep Not Just Tall. She has also produced a 60 minute audio cassette tape that is based on a presentation of her first book, Where Have All the Children Gone? Gone to Grown-Ups, Everyone! Married to her best friend, Lou Clark, she is the mother of their two children, Kelli and Kevin.

ILLUSTRATOR

Larry W. Anderson is a sculptor, painter, and art consultant living in Tacoma, Washington, with his wife, Sharilyn, and their three children. A graduate of Central Washington State University, Larry received his Master of Fine Arts from Cranbrook Art Academy in Bloomfield Hills, Michigan. He has studied at the Academy of Fine Art in Vienna, and recently opened a second studio near Paris. Widely acclaimed for his life-sized bronze sculptures depicting themes of relationships, Larry is a long time, personal friend of the author. The quote inscribed in Larry's portfolio well describes this gentle man, "We do what we can. We give what we have."

CEP PUBLICATIONS

BOOKS

Grow Deep Not Just Tall
By Karen Kaiser Clark

Where Have All The Children Gone?
Gone To Grown-Ups, Everyone!
By Karen Kaiser Clark

With sensitivity and enthusiastic humor, this book looks at the adult world through the eyes of a child. Delightfully illustrated, it challenges the reader to revitalize the following essentials so as to live more fully and to become more real:

1) Sense of Wonder
2) Excitement for Living
3) Freedom to Choose
4) Admitting Vulnerability
5) Self Acceptance
6) Mystery in Life

TAPE

A 60 Minute Audio Cassette Tape
Featuring Karen Kaiser Clark

This presentation is based on her book, Where Have All the Children Gone? Gone to Grown-Ups, Everyone! Recorded before a live audience, you will hear the wit, wisdom and warmth of Karen Kaiser Clark as only she can communicate.

For information on the availability of Karen Kaiser Clark as a keynote speaker or consultant for your organization, contact The Center for Executive Planning, Inc., 13119 Heritage Way, Suite 1200, St. Paul, Minnesota 55124. Telephone: 612/454-1163